Teaching and Learning
Key Stage 2
Differentiated Activity Book

Word

FOUNTAINS C.E. SCHOOL

Literacy

Year 6

Contents

 # Introduction

Differentiated Activity Books:

- support the teaching of the Literacy Hour
- help meet the majority of the objectives of the National Literacy Strategy Framework
- contain 30 units of work, sufficient for one school year
- are straightforward and easy to use
- have a clear teaching focus
- contain differentiated activities for each objective at foundation, intermediate and challenging levels of difficulty.

Features of the Word Level Teaching Units

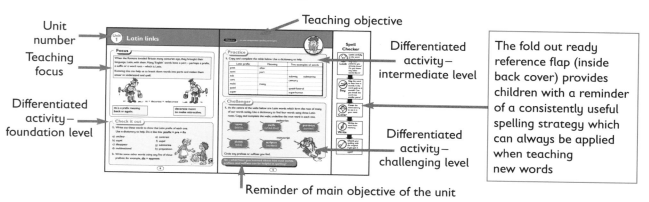

Unit number

Teaching focus

Differentiated activity — foundation level

Teaching objective

Differentiated activity — intermediate level

Differentiated activity — challenging level

Reminder of main objective of the unit

The fold out ready reference flap (inside back cover) provides children with a reminder of a consistently useful spelling strategy which can always be applied when teaching new words

Using the Differentiated Activity Books

A Variety of Uses

The books may be used to:
- introduce and teach individual National Literacy Strategy Framework objectives independently
- introduce individual National Literacy Strategy Framework objectives prior to studying them during Text Level work
- consolidate, develop and extend National Literacy Strategy Framework objectives studied during Text Level work
- provide work for whole class, group or individual work
- provide work for follow-up homework assignments.

Class Work

The Teaching focus provides a clear explanation of each objective with examples for discussion. Appropriate activities may be chosen from the range of differentiated tasks for discussion, or to work through, with the class.

Group and Individual Work

The Differentiated Activity Books are ideal for group and individual work. Work on the same objective may be realistically matched appropriately to individual children's abilities, allowing children to work independently.

Homework

The material in the books provides an ideal solution to meaningful homework assignments that can be differentiated appropriately for each pupil.

Focus

When the Romans invaded Britain many centuries ago, they brought their language, Latin, with them. Many 'English' words have a part – perhaps a prefix, a suffix or a word root – which is Latin.

Knowing this can help us to break down words into parts and makes them easier to understand and spell.

re + decorate = redecorate

re is a prefix meaning **back** or **again**.

decorate means **to make attractive**.

Check it out

1. Write out these words to show the Latin prefix of each one. Use a dictionary to help. Do it like this: <u>pre</u>fix = pre + fix

a) unclear

b) expel

c) disappear

d) multinational

e) contract

f) extinct

g) submarine

h) preposition

2. Write some other words using any five of the prefixes used above, for example, <u>dis</u> + approve

Practice

1. Copy and complete the table below. Use a dictionary to help.

Latin prefix	Meaning	Two examples of words
post	after	
semi	part	
sub		subway submarine
cent		century
multi	many	
quad		quadrilateral
super		superhuman

Challenger

1. At the centre of the webs below are Latin words which form the root of many of our words today. Use a dictionary to find four words using these Latin roots. Copy and complete the webs, underlining the root word in each one.

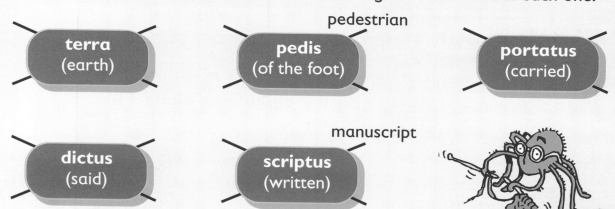

pedestrian

terra
(earth)

pedis
(of the foot)

portatus
(carried)

manuscript

dictus
(said)

scriptus
(written)

Circle any prefixes or suffixes you find.

So – what have you learned about how root words, prefixes and suffixes can be helpful in spelling?

Focus

When the Romans invaded Britain, they brought words from Ancient Greece, as well as Latin. In the fifteenth century, using Greek became very fashionable, so more words were used. Many 'English' words have a part – perhaps a prefix, a suffix or a word root – which is Greek.

Knowing this can help us to break down words into parts and makes them easier to understand and spell.

syn + onoma = synonym

A **synonym** is a word which has the same meaning:
syn is a prefix meaning **with** or **together**
onoma meant **a name**

Check it out

1. Write out these words to show the Greek prefix of each one.
   Use a dictionary to help. Do it like this: **alphabet = alpha + bet**

a) antonym

b) biology

c) geology

d) homonym

e) telephone

f) photograph

g) hippopotamus

h) microphone

i) television

j) paragraph

2. Write some other words using any five of these prefixes, for example, **geo** + **graphy**

Practice

1. Copy and complete the table below. Use a dictionary to help.

Greek prefix	Meaning	Two examples of words
bio	life	biology
tele	far	
geo		geography geometry
photo		photograph
micro		microscope
demos	people	
mono	single	
poly	many	

Challenger

1. At the centre of the webs below are Greek words which form the root of many of our words today. Use a dictionary to find four words using these Greek roots. Underline the root word in each one. Circle any prefixes or suffixes you find.

cycle

anti
(against)

cyclos
(circle)

para
(beyond)

thermos
(heat)

logy
(word, study)

So – what have you learned about how word roots, prefixes and suffixes can be helpful in spelling?

Focus

Our **language** is always **changing**. Some words remain from centuries ago, but others have disappeared or their meaning has changed.

We no longer use words such as **thou**. We use **you**.

Nice used to mean **fussy** or **precise**.

Check it out

1. Copy and complete this table to show how words connected with the cinema and with music have changed in meaning. Use a dictionary.

Word	Used to mean only	Today's extra meaning
shot	Shot from a gun	One photograph
rock	A rock on the ground	
still	Not moving	
album	To put photographs in	
film	A thin covering	
band	A strip to hold together	
pop	A loud sound	
location	A special place	

Practice

1. These words have all changed their meaning over time. Use a dictionary to link them up with their old meaning. Write what they mean today.

awful	a peasant
terrific	fussy
horrid	food
villain	worth nothing
nice	causing terror
meat	rough, bristly
naughty	full of wonder

2. Write some sentences using five of the words to show what they mean today.

Challenger

1. Here is a passage from a poem written in 1390, describing a man who looked after a knight. Rewrite it in modern English, using the key for help.

> Of twenty yeer of age he was, I gesse.
> Of his stature he was of evene length,
> And wonderly delyvere and of great strengthe…
> Syngynge he was or floytynge al the day;
> He was as fressh as is the month of May.
> Short was his gowne, with sleves long and wyde.
> Wel koude he sitte on hor and fair ryde.

Key

stature – height
delyvere – lively
floytynge – playing the flute
gowne – outfit

The Squire by Geoffrey Chaucer

a) Which words can you recognise from six hundred years ago?

b) Which words have changed?

So – what have you learned about how words and expressions have changed over time?

Unit 4 Origins of names

Focus

Looking at the place where you live, your own surname, or even the days of the week, may help you to spell words.

Oxford. A **ford** is a place to cross a river. The town was named Oxford because it was a place where oxen used to do this.

If someone has the surname **Smith,** then they are relatives of people who were blacksmiths hundreds of years ago.

Wednesday is a difficult word to spell, but may seem easier if you know it was named after the Anglo-Saxon God **Woden**. So it is really **Woden's day**.

Check it out

1. Copy and complete the table below. Match the days of the week with their derivation. Check your spelling in a dictionary.

Day of the week	Derivation	Original meaning
Monday	The day of the god Woden	Moon's day
	The day of the god Thor	
	The day of the god of the Sun	
	The day of the goddess Tiw	
	The day of the moon	
	The day of the goddess Frig	
	The day of the god Saturn	

Practice

1. People were often named after where they lived.

Explain how these people might have got their names.

> Hill   Moor   Townsend   Field   Meadows

Add one more name to the list which was derived in the same way.

2. People were often named after their work, or what they did.

Explain how these people might have got their names.

> Thatcher   Tanner   Clark   Baker   Smith

Add one more name to the list which was derived in the same way.

3. People were sometimes named after their families.

Explain how these people might have got their names. (You may need to use a special dictionary for the final two examples.)

> Johnson   Redhead   Long   MacDonald   O'Neil

Add one more name to the list which was derived in the same way.

Challenger

1. The Anglo-Saxons named many places in Britain. Use an atlas to find places containing these Anglo-Saxon words and describe how they got their names.

Do it like this: **Birm – ing – ham = the village of the people of Birm**

> **ing** – people of that place
> **ton, tun** – a farming place
> **ford** – a place to cross a river
> **minster** – a place where there was a church
> **chester, caster** – a place where there was a Roman fort
>
> **ham** – a village or hamlet
> **stead** – the place of
> **bourne** – a stream

So – what have you learned about the origins of proper names?

Focus

Our language is **constantly changing**. New words are added all the time as new things are invented.

People did not use the word **trainer** until training shoes became popular a few years ago.

Nobody used the term **supermarket** until this kind of shopping became popular in America.

Check it out

1. As computers become more important, we have added more new 'computer words' to our language. Fill in the missing letters in these computer words and write out the words in your book.

   CD R_m   d_ _k   mon_ _or   k_ _boa_d

   flo_ _y di_k   m_ _se   mod_ _ _   c_rs_r

   e-ma_ _   ho_e pa_e   In_ _ _ _net   w_b s_ _e

2. Write some sentences using four of these words to show you know what they mean.

Practice

1. Look up these 'new' words in a dictionary and write out each word and its definition in your book.

stereo	helicopter	turbo	apartheid
motorway	make-up	mail order	Walkman
supermarket	nylon	disc jockey	checkout
self-service	radar	comprehensive school	

2. Now write the words in some sentences to show you know what they mean.

Challenger

1. The words below are all to do with the people who invented something. Use a dictionary to find out who the inventors were and what they invented.

a) pasteurise
b) cardigan
c) Fahrenheit
d) saxophone
e) Braille

f) Wellington
g) watt
h) biro
i) volt
j) newton

2. Choose four inventors from the list above. Write a sentence about each of their inventions.

So – what have you learned about how new words have been added to the language?

Focus

An etymological dictionary is one that tells you about the origins of words. Look at the extract below. **Etymology** comes from an Ancient Greek word meaning **the true sense of a word**.

etumon + logia = etymology

(**etumon** – true)   (**logia** – of words)

Alphabet The first two Greek letters are **alpha** and **beta**. Originally the set of letters used in writing the Greek language. Now any set of letters representing the simple sounds of language.

Biscuit From the Latin **bis (twice)** and **coctus (cooked)**. To keep them fresh, biscuits used to be baked twice to make them hard.

Dandelion From the French **dent de lion** – 'lion's tooth'. It describes the jagged edges of the leaves.

Nickname From the Anglo-Saxon **Ekename**. **Eke** means **also**. A name that is used instead of the proper name of a person.

Check it out

1. Look at the 'Focus' section again. Answer these questions in your book.

a) What is an etymological dictionary?
b) How is the word **etymology** derived?
c) From which language does **alphabet** originally come?
d) From which two words does **alphabet** come?
e) Explain how the word **biscuit** came to be invented.
f) From which language does **dandelion** come?
g) How did the plant get this name?
h) From which language does **nickname** come?
i) How is it linked with the word **also**?

Practice

1. Use a dictionary to find the origin of these words.
Write them in the correct column in the table.

> microphone   dungarees   automatic   caravan   theology
> bungalow   physics   kiosk   pharmacy   thug
> pyjamas   punch   sugar   cot   lilac

Words from Persian	Words from Greek	Words from Hindi
caravan		

2. Now write some sentences using any two words from each column.

Challenger

1. Carry out research to find how these words came into our language.
Look at the clues in the box.

a) juggernaut   c) teddy bear   e) sandwich

b) marathon   d) hooligan

> • Ancient Greek battle story
> • huge Hindi statue dragged through streets every year
> • US president refused to kill animal
> • nineteenth-century Irish family in London known to be disorderly
> • Earl who invented a snack so he would not have to stop playing cards

So – what have you learned about using an etymological dictionary?

Focus

Mnemonics are tricks we use to help us **remember something**.

Never **E**at **S**hredded **W**heat helps us to remember the points of the compass – **N**orth, **E**ast, **S**outh and **W**est.

Mnemonics are very helpful when you are trying to remember how to spell tricky words.

Wasps **A**lways **S**ting spells **WAS**.

Check it out

1. Write the words that these mnemonics will help you spell. Do it like this:
<u>**You**</u> **are young** – **YOUNG** (**You** is the word found in **young**.)

a) **D**ad **o**pens **e**very **S**aturday

b) A piece of **pie**

c) I will be your friend until the **end**

d) **U**-turn

e) **Al** walked and talked

f) It's great to **eat**

g) It's busy on the **bus**

h) **U and I** build the wall

i) **M**other **a**pes **n**ever **y**awn

Practice

1. Think of some mnemonics to help you spell these words,

important

| i _____ |
| m _____ |
| p _____ |
| o _____ |
| r _____ |
| t _____ |
| a _____ |
| n _____ |
| t _____ |

vegetable

| v _____ |
| e _____ |
| g _____ |
| e _____ |
| t _____ |
| a _____ |
| b _____ |
| l _____ |
| e _____ |

secretary

| s _____ |
| e _____ |
| c _____ |
| r _____ |
| e _____ |
| t _____ |
| a _____ |
| r _____ |
| y _____ |

immediate

| i _____ |
| m _____ |
| m _____ |
| e _____ |
| d _____ |
| i _____ |
| a _____ |
| t _____ |
| e _____ |

Challenger

1. Looking for words inside words can often help you to invent mnemonics, for example: **<u>land</u> is found in is<u>land</u>, so a mnemonic could be We <u>land</u> on the is<u>land</u>.**

Underline the small words inside these long words. Write a mnemonic for each word which will help you to remember how to spell them. The first one has been done for you.

a) <u>restaurant</u>

b) chocolate

c) together

d) teacher

e) separate

f) introduction

g) temperature

h) elephant

i) height

j) juice

So – what have you learned about mnemonics?

Focus

ible and **able** are common letter strings.

Letter strings are groups of letters which you find in words.

The meaning of the suffixes **ible** and **able** is **able to** or **fit for**.

laugh ⟶ laughable   invis ⟶ invisible

Generally, **able** is added to a whole word.
ible is added when the word root is not a whole word.

Check it out

1. Copy the sentences below. Circle any **ible** or **able** letter strings.
The first one has been done for you.

a) There has been a terrible accident.

b) On the television it said that the weather would be changeable.

c) Our mission was impossible to carry out.

d) That attempt at singing a song was laughable.

e) After he had finished sewing, the rip was invisible.

f) That is a very fashionable mountain bike.

g) Dean's report from the school was very favourable.

2. Where do the **ible** and **able** letter strings always occur – the beginning, middle or ends of words?

Practice

1. Add **ible** or **able** to these word roots. Write the words. Underline the word roots.
What do you notice about them?

> accept
> favour
> notice
> laugh
> fashion
> understand
>
> **+ ible** or **able?**

2. Add **ible** or **able** to these word roots. Write the words. Underline the word roots.
What do you notice about them?

> terr
> poss
> invis
> divis
> incred
> vis
>
> **+ ible** or **able?**

Challenger

1. Add **ible** or **able** to these words. Use a dictionary to help.
   a) rely   b) envy   c) justify
   What happens? Write a rule to explain it.

2. Add **ible** or **able** to these words. Use a dictionary to help.
   a) love   b) believe
   What happens? Write a rule to explain it.

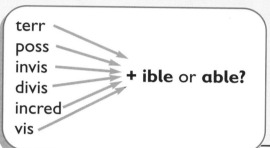

3. Add **ible** or **able** to these words. Use a dictionary to help.
   a) change   b) knowledge   c) manage
   What happens? Write a rule to explain it.

4. Words such as **corruptible, collapsible, despicable, applicable** are all exceptions to the rules. How?
   Use a dictionary to find two more words which are exceptions.

So – what have you learned about spelling words containing 'ible' and 'able'?

Focus

Some **letter combinations** make the **same sound**.

This can make words difficult to spell!

Think about words that contain the same sound as in **ou**ch.

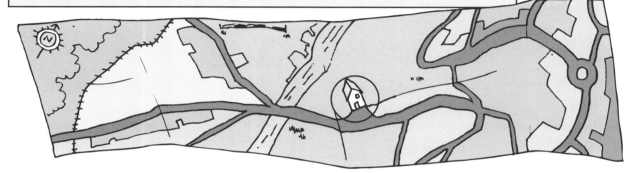

Our **house** is in the centre of **town**.

This Unit will help you come to some conclusions about this.

Check it out

1. Copy the sentences below. Circle all the words which contain the same **sound** as in **ouch!** The first one has been done for you.

a) It was bound to happen in the end.

b) He nearly drowned in the fast-flowing river.

c) The Trevi fountain in Rome is very famous.

d) Take the towel into the shower.

e) He saw the owl fly into the tower.

f) Your trousers will be ready in an hour, Sir.

g) What do you do if you find a mouse in your house?

2. How many different groups of letters make the sound? What are they? Write a list.

Practice

1. Sort the words in the box into two columns according to the letter string that makes the **ouch!** sound. Label the other column.

ouch!	bound	found	shower	owl
amount	house	drown	brown	towel
around	mountain	mouse	growl	flower

ou letter string	___ letter string
ouch!	

Challenger

1. Write a rule which will help to spell words containing this **ouch!** sound. Answer the questions below:

a) Which groups of letters normally come after **ou**?

b) Which letter string only comes at the end of words?

c) Write five more words to prove the rules you have just written.

2. a) Find seven **ou** or **ow** words in this wordsearch.

b) Now write some sentences using the words in your book.

t	r	o	u	t	y
l	c	r	o	w	n
o	c	o	u	n	t
u	c	l	o	w	n
d	s	h	o	u	t
x	a	l	l	o	w

So – what have you learned about spelling words with similar letter patterns?

Focus

A **polysyllabic word** is a word with **more than one syllable**. Sometimes, **vowels** in these words are **not always stressed**, or pronounced as you would expect, and so they become difficult to spell.

carpet   interest

The **e** in each word often gets missed out.

Check it out

1. Write out these words, putting in the missing vowels.

a) alc_h_l

b) b_s_ness

c) cem_t_ry

d) fore_gn

e) secr_t_ry

f) b_ch_lor

g) cal_nd_r

h) col_n_l

i) g_arant_e

j) sep_r_te

Practice

1. These eight difficult words have been broken into their separate syllables.
Choose a syllable from each box. Join the syllables up and write the words.

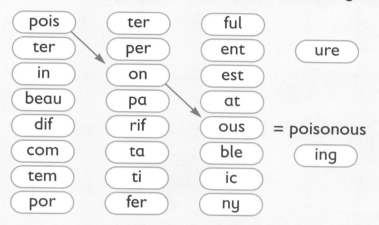

pois	ter	ful
ter	per	ent	ure
in	on	est
beau	pa	at
dif	rif	ous	= poisonous
com	ta	ble	ing
tem	ti	ic
por	fer	ny

2. Circle the vowel in each word which often gets missed out in spelling.

Challenger

1. Copy and complete the table below using the words in the box.
This will show you how knowing about the structure and derivation
of words can help you spell them.

> extraordinary   practice   signature   celebration   temperature
> independent   description   stationary freedom   different.

Root of the word	A possible prefix	A possible suffix
ordinary	extra	

So – what have you learned about spelling patterns
for unstressed vowels in polysyllabic words?

23

Focus

Mnemonics are tricks we use to help us **remember something**. Mnemonics are very helpful when you are trying to remember how to spell tricky words.

Wasps **A**lways **S**ting spells **WAS**.

Check it out

1. Match the mnemonic to the word it will help you to spell. Write out the mnemonic and the word. Look for the clues (the capital letters in the words).

Mnemonics	Words
Don't make me ANGry. I'm …	teacher
I like PIE. Give me a …	government
He ATE it all. My …	temperature
There's a RAT in …	chocolate
They GOVERN.	piece
They're a pain. They contain an ACHE.	dangerous

Practice

1. Write a mnemonic to help you spell these words. Read each word downwards.

February	Miniature	Twelfth	Wednesday
F _____	m _____	t _____	W _____
e _____	i _____	w _____	e _____
b _____	n _____	e _____	d _____
r _____	i _____	l _____	n _____
u _____	a _____	f _____	e _____
a _____	t _____	t _____	s _____
r _____	u _____	h _____	d _____
y _____	r _____		a _____
	e _____		y _____

2. Check the derivation of the four words above in a dictionary to help you remember them, for example, the prefix in **mini**ature is **mini**, meaning **small**.

Challenger

1. Write out these difficult words. Underline the small words inside the long words. The first one has been done for you.

a) is<u>land</u>

b) wonderful

c) height

d) ghost

e) vegetable

f) together

g) geography

h) practice

i) juice

j) because

Write a mnemonic for each word which will help you remember how to spell them.

So – what have you learned about mnemonics?

Focus

We can understand why words are spelled in a particular way if we can understand their **origin** and **derivation** – where they came from originally.

Telephone comes from two Greek words.

Tele means **from afar**   **phone** means **sound.**

tele + phone

Knowing these Greek prefixes and roots now helps us to understand the meaning of and spell other words, for example, **television** means being able to **see from afar**.

Check it out

1. Each word in Box A is connected with a particular number.
   Match each word in Box A with a number in Box B and write both out. Do it like this: **uniform – uni (one)**. Use a dictionary to help.

Box A

<u>uni</u>form	triangle
decimal	quarter
century	millennium
octet	bicycle
pentagon	unique

Box B

<u>one</u>	two
three	four
five	eight
ten	one
one hundred	
one thousand	

Practice

1. Copy and complete the table below. Use your dictionary to help.

Prefix	Meaning	Two examples using the prefix	
tri			
sub		subset	subtitle
dis			
trans	across		
poly	many		
anti			
auto		automatic	

Challenger

1. Make your own dictionary of these new words. Write where
you think the words might be derived from.
Many of these words will not yet be in your dictionary.

wheelie	trailer
backing track	bucket shop
nerd	teenager
disc jockey	mail order
one-armed	bandit
self-service	developing country
comprehensive school	Playstation

So – what have you learned about the origin and derivation of words?

Focus

Proverbs are **well known sayings**.
They often try to **teach us a lesson** by using ideas we recognise to get the message across.

> While the cat's away, the mice will play.

This proverb is not really about cats and mice, it is about how people take advantage of a situation to have fun.

Check it out

1. Copy the sentences below and underline the proverbs.
The first one has been done for you.

a) When I would not save, my mother always told me <u>to take care of the pennies and the pounds would take care of themselves.</u>

b) When I was celebrating winning the match, Fred said, "Don't count your chickens before they hatch."

c) He was always boasting but I reminded myself that empty vessels make the most sound.

d) When she laughed because I did not pass the test, I told her to be careful because people who live in glass houses shouldn't throw stones.

e) "Better late than never," said the teacher when I handed in my homework.

f) Don't risk everything. Be careful and look before you leap.

g) She only paid me back half my money, but I did not complain as half a loaf is better than none.

h) She left me the car to use, so I decided to make hay while the sun shines!

Practice

1. Join the two halves of these proverbs together. Write them out correctly in your book.

While the cat's away	spoil the broth.
A stitch in time	and eat it, too.
A rolling stone	is worth two in the bush.
A fool and his money	make light work.
Never judge a book	by its cover.
Many hands	are soon parted.
A bird in the hand	gathers no moss.
You can't have your cake	saves nine.
Too many cooks	the mice will play.

Challenger

1. Take each of the proverbs in the 'Check it out' and 'Practice' sections and use them to make a Proverbs Dictionary.
Add two more proverbs of your own.

Remember:

- you will need to put them into alphabetical order
- you will need to give their meanings
- you could investigate where the proverbs originated.

So – what have you learned about the meanings and origins of proverbs?

Focus

English is a language which **continually changes**. Words which used to mean one thing many years ago now mean something completely different.

In the 1590s, Shakespeare wrote:

Thou naughty knave

This was almost an insult. **Naughty** meant **less than naught** (or nothing). If we used the word today, it would mean someone who behaves in a silly way.

Check it out

1. Each of the words below has two meanings which have developed over time. Look up the words in your dictionary and write both meanings.

a) fence

b) strike

c) coach

d) mint

e) bulb

f) score

Practice

1. The words and phrases below have all come to mean something new.
   Look in your dictionary to find the most modern meanings.
   (Look at the clues in brackets.)

a) comprehensive (education)

b) trainer (shoe)

c) receiver (phone)

d) bucket (seat)

e) mouse (computer)

f) jet (plane)

g) boot (car)

h) jockey (music)

i) still (photo)

j) screen (film)

2. What did each word used to mean? Write the original meaning
   alongside the new meaning.

Challenger

1. Copy this passage from the story of the prodigal son in the Bible. This was
   how it was written in 1611. Notice how, in some words, the letters **u** and the **v**
   are muddled up.

> His elder sonne was in the field and as he came and drew nigh to the
> house he heard musicke and dauncing and he called one of the
> seruants and asked what these things meant. And he said vnto him,
> Thy brother is come, and thy father hath killed the fatted calfe because
> he hath receiued him safe and sound.

a) Underline the words which are spelled differently from words today but
   which you can recognise.

b) Circle the words which we do not use today.

c) Write a version in modern English.

So – what have you learned about meanings changing over time?

Focus

Longer words can be broken down into **smaller parts** called **syllables**.

Bad has one syllable.   **Bad/min/ton** has three syllables.

- Each syllable must contain at least one vowel sound (which could be **y**).
- Syllables do not have to make whole words by themselves.
- You can make new words from separate syllables.

Compound words are words made up of **complete other words**, for example, **any + one = anyone** or **black + berry = blackberry**

Check it out

1. Take a word from each box to make a compound word.
   Write each word. Say how many syllables each word contains.
   Do it like this:
   football (2 syllables)

2. Now write five more compound words of your own. Say how many syllables each word contains.

foot	man
snow	band
head	ground
play	box
post	ball
night	mare
rain	bow
farm	yard
birth	day
head	ache

Practice

1. Join up one syllable from each column to make complete words.
Write out the words in your book.

al	er	dar	
cal	per	ary	le
ex	to	ab	
gov	u	geth	ure
tem	ess	ar	
val	uc	ment	ion
ed	ru	at	
dic	tion	ary	y
nec	en	at	er = altogether
Feb	ern	cise	

Challenger

1. Add the missing vowels to these words from Ancient Egypt. Check the
meanings of the words in a dictionary or a history book if you are unsure.
Write how many syllables are in each word, for example, **Egypt (2).**

a) pyr_m_d

b) m_mmy

c) t_mb

d) ls_s

e) sh_d_f

f) phar___h

g) h__roglyphs

h) T_t_nkh_mun

i) p_pyr_s

j) scr_be

k) ob_lisk

l) Nilom_t_r

m) inund_t_on

n) t_mple

o) pr___stess

p) Os_r_s

q) Theb_s

r) inscr_pt_on

s) lin_n

t) Cl__patra

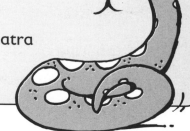

So – what have you learned about syllables?

Focus

A **phoneme** is the **smallest unit of sound** in a word.

c – a – t has three phonemes.

eye – s has two phonemes.

Sometimes, the same phoneme can make a different sound in a word, for example, **root** and **blood**.

Check it out

1. Copy the word sets. Underline the letters which each word has in common.

a) marry   party   star   market

b) snowing   now   bowl   know

c) call   small   stall   shall

d) waste   ask   pass   disaster

e) pouring   hour   course   four

f) earth   early   dear   rehearse

Now circle the word which sounds different in each set.

Practice

1. Copy these boxes in your book. Add two more words to each box
which use the **same phoneme** and make the **same sound**. Then
write a word which uses the same phoneme but makes a **different
sound**, like the first one.

tr**ea**t   s**ea**t

Different sound: b**ea**r

fl**oa**t

Different sound:

s**oo**n

Different sound:

p**ai**n

Different sound:

c**ou**gh

Different sound:

f**ie**ld

Different sound:

Use one word from each box in a sentence to show you know what it means.

Challenger

1. Find five words which have the same phoneme as each of the underlined
phonemes in the boxes below. The first one has been started.
Remember – these do not have to be spelled the same!

sh**oe**
two
thr**ough**

c**ould**

st**ay**

d**i**rty

h**or**se

cl**ou**d

Use one word from each box in a sentence.

So – what have you learned about spelling rules and exceptions?

Focus

The same consonant may sound different in different words, like **cemetery** and **cat.**

The letter following the consonant makes them sound this way. Some consonants drop a letter, like

I am **full** of hope ➝ I am **hopeful**

Some consonants double when you word-build, like **pop** and **popper**.

This unit should help you to make some rules which will help you with these consonant problems.

Cemetery Cat

Check it out

1. Decide whether the words in the box contain **hard** or **soft c** and **g**.
   Copy and complete the table using those words.

Soft sound – **c** or **g**	Hard sound – **c** or **g**
cellar	

great	cellar	disguise	chord	ceiling
goalkeeper	cottage	manager	cupboard	change
guess	ranger	gift	centre	ghost

Which letters coming before or after the **c** or **g** make them have this sound?

Practice

1. Decide if you spell these words with a double **l** or not.

a) Add the suffix **full** or **ful** to these words in order to spell them correctly.

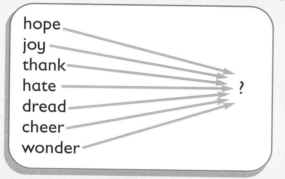

hope
joy
thank
hate
dread
cheer
wonder

?

b) Add the prefix **all** or **al** to these words in order to spell them correctly.

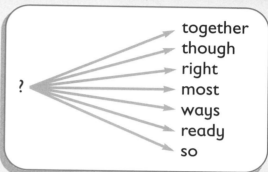

?

together
though
right
most
ways
ready
so

c) Write a rule which will help you to remember what happens when you spell the words in this section.

Challenger

1. a) Decide if words should double their final consonant when you word-build. Copy and complete the table. Write all the words you can make. For example, **hop, hopper, hopped.**

b) Write a rule about when you should double the final consonant of single syllable words.

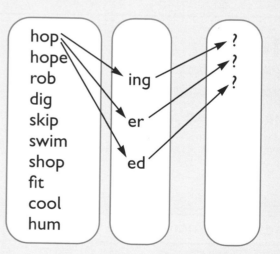

hop
hope
rob
dig
skip
swim
shop
fit
cool
hum

ing
er
ed

?
?
?

So – what have you learned about spelling rules for consonants?

Unit 18 Vowels

Focus

The same **vowels** may sound **different** in different words.
These are called **long** and **short vowel sounds**.

 sign    fin

Some vowels, such as **i** and **e** can cause confusion when spelling.

 c**e**iling   beli**e**ve

Other vowels, such as **e** may drop when you word-build.

writ**e** writing

Check it out

1. Copy and complete the table below about long and short vowel sounds.
Find and write pairs of the words from the box in the correct columns.

hope	pet	rob	mat	Pete	fin	made
fine	apple	hop	mate	ape	Pope	gap
tube	pop	robe	gape	mad	tub	

Sounds like the name of the letter (long)	Sounds like the name of the letter (short)
wine	win

Which letter makes the vowel change its sound?

Practice

1. a) Decide if words should drop their final vowel when you word-build. Copy and complete these word sums. Write all the words you can make.

   b) Write a rule which will explain what happens when you add the suffixes **ing**, **er** and **ed** to words ending in **e**.

| care
write
like
hope
love
live
use
excite
arrive
describe | + | ing

er

ed | = | caring carer cared |

Challenger

1. Write out the words in the box. Add the missing letters **ei** or **ie** to them. Use a dictionary to help.

pr_ _st	rec_ _pt	br_ _f	s_ _ge	ach_ _ve	dec_ _t	sh_ _ld
rel_ _f	rec_ _ve	p_ _ce	y_ _ld	dec_ _ve	f_ _ld	h_ _r
c_ _ling	n_ _ghbour	bel_ _ve	ch_ _f	fr_ _nd	w_ _ght	th_ _r

Now sort the words into the correct columns in the table below.

ie words – sound like **ee**	**ei** words – sound like **ee**	other **ei** words

Write a rule which explains when you use **ei** or **ie** in words. What exceptions can you find to the rule?

So – what have you learned about spelling rules for vowels?

Focus

Some words are difficult to spell because they contain letters which are not pronounced – they are **silent**.

A **kn**ight is on his **kn**ees.

Many centuries ago, people used to pronounce the **k** in these words – but over time this was dropped.

Check it out

1. Copy these silly rhymes. Insert the silent letters.

> G_ostly g_ouls and
> g_astly g_osts eat
> g_oulish g_erkins.

> A _night with _nobbly _nees once
> _new how to _not while _neeling
> with a _napsack on his back.

> G_omes and g_ats
> like to g_ash and g_aw.

> The plum_er's thum_ became
> num_ as he clim_ed.

Practice

1. Read the words in the box. Identify those which have silent letters. Copy the table and add the words to the correct columns. (Some words will appear more than once.)

queen	knot	plumber	wheel	aghast	knee	lamb	wreck
climb	gnat	debt	raspberry	island	rhyme	science	wrestle
hymn	knife	chemist	thumb	listen	rabbit	write	rough
autumn	sign	gnome	ghost	whistle	honour	vehicle	should
salmon	fasten	farm	crumb	rhubarb	wriggle	rhyme	scene

Silent letter at beginning of word	Silent letter in middle of word	Silent letter at end of word

2. Now add six more words containing silent letters to the table.
Say which letters come before or after the silent letters to make them **silent**.

Challenger

1. Copy and complete the table below. Write rules which will help you to spell words with silent letters.

Silent letter	Rule	Two examples
b	Comes after **m** at the end of a syllable or a word. Also comes before **t**.	climb, debt
	Silent after **s**.	
	Comes before **n**.	
	Follows **w** and **r**. Also found at the start of words.	
	Silent before **s**, **n** or **t**.	
	Sometimes silent in front of **h**.	
	Silent after **m**.	
	Sometimes silent in front of **d**, **k** and **m**.	

So – what have you learned about spelling rules for silent letters?

41

Focus

Thesaurus comes from a Greek word for **treasury** or **storehouse**. You use a thesaurus to find a word which means **the same as** (a synonym).

We can use a theasaurus so we do not use the same words time and again.

When you choose a word from a thesaurus, you need to be careful about how it is going to be used in the sentence.

Beat   (verb) to strike, hit, pound, thrash, batter, knock, thwack, thump, pound, hammer (noun) a blow, a throb.

Combat (verb) to withstand, oppose, battle, fight, resist (noun) a war, conflict, struggle, fight, battle, action.

Hot   (adjective) tropical, steamy, sticky, sunny, spicy, boiling, baking, blistering, fiery, sizzling, sweltering.

Little   (adjective) small, tiny, brief, short, trivial, slight, mean, selfish.

Check it out

1. Look at the 'Focus' section again.
   Answer these questions.

a) What does the word **thesaurus** mean?

b) What do you use a thesaurus for?

c) How is it different from a dictionary?

d) Write one synonym for the verb **to beat** and one for the word as a noun.

e) Write one synonym for the verb **to combat** and one for the word as a noun.

f) Write two synonyms for **hot** which would best describe a cup of tea.

g) Which two synonyms for **hot** would not be good to describe a cup of tea. Why?

h) Which synonyms for **little** would you use to describe how someone looked?

i) Which synonyms for **little** would you use to describe someone's character?

Practice

1. Use a thesaurus to find five more synonyms for each of these words:

> look
>
> hear
>
> touch
>
> smell
>
> taste

2. Choose one of the examples. Write the words in sentences to show you understand the differences in their meaning.

Challenger

1. Avoid using words such as **nice**. Use a thesaurus to rewrite these phrases. Replace **nice** with a more interesting word each time.

a) a nice person

b) a nice house

c) a nice drink

d) a nice bike

e) a nice book

f) a nice dream

2. Find five synonyms for the word **said**, for example, **shouted** or **whispered**. Write them in sentences to show the differences in their meaning.

3. Use a thesaurus to explain the difference between the words in each group below.

a) stroll   wander   ramble

b) news   rumour   scandal

c) firm   obstinate   pig-headed

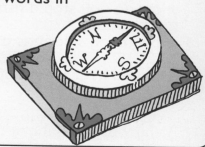

So – what have you learned about using a thesaurus?

Focus

Language is fun! **Playing with words** can make you see the differences in words.

> What did the fish say to his girlfriend?

> Come back to my plaice!

Playing with words can make you look more closely at them.
Did you know that **star** is **rats** backwards?

Check it out

1. The jokes below are all muddled up. Match the joke beginnings
with their punchlines.
   Write out the jokes and punctuate them correctly as questions and answers.

How do you make a band stand?	A rubbish lorry.
What do you get when you cross a giraffe with a hedgehog?	Two – an inside and an outside.
What has four wheels and flies?	It blew away.
How do you stop a fish from smelling?	A four metre toothbrush.
How many sides has a football?	Because restaurants don't usually serve fish.
Did you hear what happened to the paper shop?	Twelve. January second, February second …
Why was the hungry cod angry?	Take away the chairs.
How many seconds in a year?	Chop off its nose.

Practice

1. Solve the anagrams below and write out the new words. (The clues in brackets might help you.) Do it like this: **melon – lemon**

a) lime (a distance)

b) star (rodent)

c) step (nuisance)

d) wolves (not consonants)

e) sword (what you write)

f) plate (on a flower)

g) cheap (a fruit)

h) ocean (small boat)

i) lamp (on your hand)

2. Now make up five anagrams of animal names to test a friend.

Challenger

1. Change one letter at a time to make new words in the wall.

Do it like this: **h<u>i</u>m ⟶ h<u>e</u>m ⟶ he<u>r</u>**

a) warm	_____	card	_____	cold				
b) car	_____	bat	_____	bus				
c) boy	_____	lay	_____					
d) hard	_____	cart	_____	_____	sort	_____		
e) rug	_____	_____	mat					
f) west	_____	_____	east					
g) wet	_____	pat	_____	_____	dry			
h) two	_____	_____	_____	_____	six			

So – what have you learned about language from playing word games?

Focus

Language is fun! **Playing with words** can make you see the differences in words.

What did the salad say when it rang the door bell?

Lettuce in!

Playing with words can make you look more closely at them.
Did you know that **mug** is **gum** backwards?

Check it out

1. Rewrite this tongue-twister. Put in the full stops and capital letters, as necessary.

What makes the passage difficult to say?

betty bought a bit of butter
betty said, "my butter's bitter
if I put it in my batter
it will make my batter bitter
better buy some better butter"
betty's mother said she'd let her
so she bought some better butter
and it made her batter better

Practice

1. Put the letters of each word in a different order, making two anagrams for each word. Do it like this: **team = meat, tame**

a) flow

b) tea

c) evil

d) peal

e) slime

f) stop

g) time

h) slate

2. Now make up five anagrams of car names to test a friend.

Challenger

1. Change one letter at a time to make new words in the wall.
Do it like this: **p<u>i</u>n ➞ p<u>e</u>n ➞ <u>h</u>en**

a) cat _____ _____ dog

b) soft _____ port _____ cart

c) some _____ cone _____

d) well _____ sill _____ sick

e) day _____ pat _____ wet

f) cold _____ _____ head _____

g) five _____ find _____ _____ lead

h) new _____ fed _____ _____ _____ and _____ odd _____

So – what have you learned about language from playing word games?

Focus

A **polysyllabic word** is a word with **more than one syllable**.
Sometimes, vowels in these words are not always stressed, or
pronounced, and so they become difficult to spell.
For example, in **company**, the **a** is often not stressed and so is left out.

Check it out

1. Match the clues to the words. Write in the missing vowels.

Clues	Words
The day after Tuesday	veg_tables
Measure it with a thermometer	temp_rature
Shows months and days	Febru_ry
Sweet made from cocoa beans	min_ature
It follows January	gen_ral
Buy them at a greengrocer	choc_late
In charge of an army	cal_ndar
Something tiny	Wedn_sday

Practice

1. Break the words in the box into their syllables and write them out.

   Do it like this: **val + u + able**

   Circle the vowels. Do it like this: **v ⓐl + ⓤ + ⓐb l ⓔ**

   | vacuum   extraordinary   diamond   factory   beautiful   business |
   | independent   carpet   celebration   poisonous   monastery |

2. Now write the words in the correct column in the table.

2 syllables	3 syllables	4 syllables	5 syllables
	valuable		

Challenger

1. Find ten words of more than one syllable in the wordsearch.
   These words contain vowels that are often missed out.
   Write out the words.

c	e	m	e	t	e	r	y	a	d
b	c	s	e	p	a	r	a	t	e
s	e	c	r	e	t	a	r	y	s
d	j	r	k	s	l	t	m	u	c
v	y	c	o	m	p	a	n	y	r
e	n	w	n	x	o	z	p	a	i
i	n	t	e	r	e	s	t	g	p
f	i	m	p	o	r	t	a	n	t
d	i	f	f	e	r	e	n	t	i
h	q	f	r	e	e	d	o	m	o
p	o	r	t	a	b	l	e	i	n

2. Make up mnemonics to help you to spell the words you found. For example, a hot **temper** gives a **temper**ature.

So – what have you learned about unstressed vowels in polysyllabic words?

Focus

Similes are comparisons. They use words such as like or as to compare things.

She swam **like** a fish.

He is **as** thin **as** a twig.

Check it out

1. Copy the sentences below. Underline the similes and circle the word in each sentence which tells you it is a simile. The first one has been done for you.

a) The trees were (as) straight (as) pillars.

b) The gold medal winner ran like a cheetah.

c) The sky was as black as coal.

d) She sang like a nightingale.

e) His face was as red as a tomato.

f) The wind cut through me like a knife.

g) He fought the gang like a tiger.

h) The light shone as bright as a star in the night sky.

i) I shook with nerves like a leaf in the wind.

Practice

1. Join the two halves of the similes and write them out in your book.

As white as	a red beetle.
As thin as	swans floating on a lake.
The bus moved like	a sheet in a washing powder advert.
The fog drifted about like	blood on a white handkerchief.
White clouds in the sky were like	a silk scarf in the wind.
The holly berries were as red as	a lamppost.

2. Finish these similes in your own way.

a) The girls danced on stage like ...

b) Aeroplanes zoomed through the sky like ...

c) She swam across the pool like ...

Challenger

1. Copy and complete this poem. Follow the pattern of the first verse.
Add your own similes.

Think of a **bee**,
As large **as** a **tree**.

Think of a **dog**,
As _____ **as** a _____.

Think of a **fox**,
As _____ as a _____.

Think of a **bear**,
As _____ as a _____.

Think of a **cat**,
As _____ as a _____.

Think of a **snake**,
As _____ as a _____.

Now add six more lines of your own.

So – what have you learned about similes?

Focus

A **metaphor** is a **comparison of two things**. In a metaphor, we do not say that one thing is **like** another. We say it **is** something else. We use **metaphorical language**. The real meaning might mean something very different. Look at the examples and questions in the brackets.

He is an ass.
(Can he really be an animal?)

The moon is a ghostly galleon.
(Can the moon be a ship?)

Check it out

1. Copy the sentences below. Underline the metaphors, like the first one.

a) I told her that <u>her eyes were shining sapphires</u>.

b) The wind grabbed the leaves and disappeared.

c) The key to a good job is education.

d) She flew down the corridor because she was late.

e) Teachers are the backbone of our schools.

f) It was raining cats and dogs so we came home.

g) She was boiling so she took off her jumper.

h) The warrior bulldozed his way through the enemy troops.

Practice

1. Copy the sentences below. Choose a word from the brackets to make the sentences metaphors.

a) The plane (smeared, made, left) a trail of clouds across the sky.

b) The scream (came, tore, was) from her lips.

c) Tiny, sparkling (pin-pricks, stars, light-spots) twinkled in the dark night sky.

d) The torch made a (beam, finger, ray) of light in the darkness.

e) The fog (went, curled, moved) around the tree.

f) The (skeleton, shape, outline) of the tree was outlined on the hilltop.

g) The performers (moved, danced, sailed) across the stage.

h) They were greeted by (lots of, a wave of, much) applause when they finished.

2. Explain why these comparisons are metaphors and not similes.

Challenger

1. Explain the real meaning of these sentences and then how they could be used as metaphors.

For example, **He let the cat out of the bag** could be

A cat was trapped and he set him free. Used as a metaphor, it means that **he gave away a secret**.

a) He stabbed his friend in the back.

b) She remained sitting on the fence during the argument.

c) His feet were firmly planted on the ground.

d) She left no stone unturned in her search.

e) He put his shoulder to the wheel to get the job done.

So – what have you learned about metaphors?

'tion' and 'sion'

Focus

Letter strings are groups of letters which always stay the same in spelling. **tion** and **sion** are **common letter strings**. They sound very similar.

This Unit will help you to find ways to know when to use these letter strings at the ends of words.

vi**sion**   atten**tion**

Check it out

1. Add **tion** or **sion** to the ends of these words. Write the words in your book and check the meanings in a dictionary.

na
revi
sta
confu
opera
divi
invita
educa
deci

tion or **sion**

...tion?   ...sion?

Practice

1. Copy the sentences below. Write the correct word in the gap, made from the verb in brackets. Check your spelling in a dictionary. The first one has been done for you.

a) My dad told me to turn off the (to televise). **the television**

b) There was much (to confuse) after the bomb.

c) He was pleased at his (to include) in the football team.

d) The mountain had been cracked and broken by (to erode).

e) He heard the enormous (to explode) in the market place.

f) She did not pass her exam because she had done no (to revise).

g) His (to decide) was to leave the team.

h) The class was sad to hear about her (to exclude) from the school.

2. Now underline the common letter string of the words.

3. Find three more examples of verbs which can be changed using this ending. Explain how the verb changes when you use this letter string.

Challenger

1. Copy and complete this table. Underline the common letter string in the words. The first one has been done for you.

Add three more examples of your own to the table.

Verb	Noun	Changes in spelling
to operate	an operation	drop the final **e**. Add **ion**.
to invent		
to create		
to celebrate		
to relate		
to add		

So – what have you learned about recognising letter strings?

Focus

Words with double letters can be tricky to spell.

hop ➡ hopping?
or
hoping?

Check it out

1. Add **ing** to these single-syllable words.
Write out the words in your book.
Check your spelling in a dictionary.

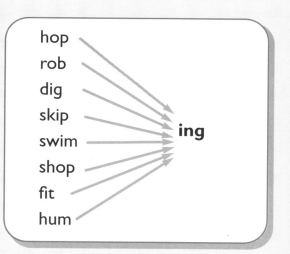

hop
rob
dig
skip
swim
shop
fit
hum

ing

2. Look at your answers to question 1. Now copy and complete this rule:
When you add a suffix to the end of a single-syllable word which has a
single vowel before the final consonant …

Practice

1. Write out the words below. Choose the correct single or double consonants from the box.

a) ac_o___

b) _u___y

c) _e__ible

d) to_o__ow

e) in_e__upt

f) di_a__ear

g) pa_a__el

h) be_i__ing

i) ne_e__ary

j) _u__est

rr	ss	rr	nn	r	pp	ss	gg	nn	f
t	m	t	s	r	g	c	rr	s	ll

2. Use five of the words from question 1 in sentences to show what they really mean.

Challenger

1. Write out these words. Choose the correct double letters from the box. (There are two in each word.)

a) su_____d

b) a__re__ive

c) a__re__

d) co__i__ee

e) po__e___

f) emba__a__

cc	gg	dd	mm	ss	ss
ee	ss	ss	tt	rr	ss

2. Now use the words in sentences to show what they really mean.

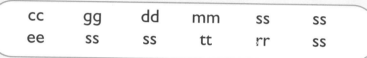

So – what have you learned about doubling letters?

57

Focus

These combinations of letters (letter strings) can sound very similar.

a teach**er**

hum**our**

a direct**or**

Check it out

1. Copy and complete these sentences in your book. All the words end
in **er** or **or**. Check your answers in a dictionary.

a) I act. I am an a_____

b) I teach. I am a t_____

c) I sing. I am a s_____

d) I invent. I am an i_____

e) I collect. I am a c_____

f) I conduct an orchestra. I am a c_____

g) I play football. I am a football p_____

h) I govern people. I am a g_____

i) I conquer people. I am a c_____

Practice

1. Copy and complete these words. Decide if they contain **er**, **or**, or **our**.
Check your answers in a dictionary.

a) carpent__

b) emper__

c) horr__

d) comput__

e) arm____

f) profess___

g) superi__

h) dang__

i) savi____

j) creat__

2. Use the words you have made in sentences to show you know what they mean.

Challenger

1. This note has been written by an American using American spelling.
Rewrite the passage using English spelling.

> I really did him a favor, but his thanks disappeared like vapor. He had no sense of humor or honor or he would have lent me the clothes. The color of the clothes he did send did not give me a sense of glamor.

2. Change these nouns to adjectives by adding the suffix **ous** like the first one. Check your spelling in a dictionary.

Noun	Adjective
danger	dangerous
adventure	
disaster	
humour	
courage	

So – what have you learned about 'er', 'or', 'our' and 'ous' words?

Focus

ge is a common **letter string**. Letter strings are groups of letters which always stay the same in spelling. The letter string **ge**, however, is often found linked to other letters.

There's a bul**ge** in the le**dge** near the cotta**ge**. It's near the fu**dge** in the fri**dge**. How stran**ge**.

This Unit will help you to find ways to know when to use these letter strings in words.

Check it out

1. Copy and complete the sentences by adding **dge**.
Underline the **dge** letter string. Circle the vowel that comes before it.

a) He saw the black and white fur of the ba____r.

b) My dad took the electric saw to cut the he____.

c) The tanks stopped before they crossed the bri____.

d) In the film the family took a lo____r into their house.

e) It was difficult to ju____ the competition.

f) Sonja gave me a nu____ and I fell off my chair.

g) We all had to do____ the cars as we crossed the road.

h) I did not bear a gru____ even though he had beaten me.

2. Say whether the vowels you have circled in each example are **long** or **short** vowels.

Practice

1. a) Add **ge** to these words. Circle the letter before **ge**.

> plun___   bul___   spon___

b) Copy and complete this sentence: A **d** is not needed before **ge** if another _____ is there.

c) Use the three words you have made in sentences.

2. a) Add **ge** to these words. Circle the letter before **ge**. What do you notice?

> an___l   stran___r   chan___
>
> dan___r   ran___   man___r

b) Use the six words you have made in sentences.

c) Say if the vowel sound is **long** or **short** in these words.

d) How is this different from the words in question 1?

Challenger

1. Exceptions occur in polysyllabic words (words with more than one syllable).

a) Add **age** or **ege** to these words. Use a dictionary to help.

> coll_____   cott_____   gar_____
>
> vill_____   all_____   coll_____

b) Find three more examples of polysyllabic words which are exceptions to what you have learned in previous sections.

c) Use any five of these words in sentences to show you know what they mean.

So – what have you learned about 'ge' words?

Focus

A **suffix** is a group of letters **added to the end of a word**.
Usually they do not change the ending of a root word.

Sometimes an **e** has to drop because the combination of letters
would make a strange sound: **write** ➔ **writ + ing**

Sometimes adding a suffix makes the final consonant double. This happens mostly
in single-syllable words: **I swim every day** ➔ **I go swim + ming everyday**

The suffix **ly** originally meant **looking like**. It is added to the whole word and,
generally, the spelling of the original word does not change: **love** ➔ **love + ly**

But it does when the words end in a y: **happy + ly** ➔ **happily**

However, **full** never appears at the end of a word: **I am full of
wonder** ➔ **I am wonder + ful**

Check it out

1. Add **ing** to these words. Write out the words in your book.
Check your answers in a dictionary.

> hope   live   arrive   write   save
> use   dive   love   like

What do you notice has happened to the final vowel?

Practice

1. a) Add **ing** to these single-syllable words. Check your answers in a dictionary.

   > run   swim   tap   beg   sit   hop   sun   rot

   What do you notice has happened to the final consonant?

   b) Copy and complete this sentence:

   In single-syllable words ending in a consonant which have a single _____ before them, the final consonant _____ when you add a suffix.

2. a) Add **ly** to these words. Check your answers in a dictionary.

   > general   fortunate   final   grateful   immediate   financial

   b) Say if anything has changed in the spelling or not.

3. a) Add **full** or **ful** to these words. Check your answers in a dictionary.

   > hope   dread   hate   peace   help   pain

   b) Now add **ly** to the words you have just made following the rule you have learned above.

Challenger

1. Copy and complete the table below using suffixes from the box.

Suffixes	Word	New word with suffix	Changes in spelling
en	lonely (adjective)	(noun) loneliness	Drop **y** – add **i** and **ness**
ment	threat (noun)	(verb)	
th	warm (adjective)	(noun)	
ship	govern (verb)	(noun)	
ness	hard (adjective)	(noun)	
dom	king (noun)	(noun)	
	strong (adjective)	(noun)	
	friend (noun)	(noun)	
	amuse (verb)	(noun)	
	free (adjective)	(noun)	
	member (noun)	(noun)	

So – what have you learned about rules for suffixing?

Range of Books Available

Year 3 Sentence	Year 4 Sentence	Year 5 Sentence	Year 6 Sentence
Year 3 Word	Year 4 Word	Year 5 Word	Year 6 Word

Literacy Differentiation Word Level Year 6

First published 1999
Reprinted 1999

Letts Educational,
9–15 Aldine Street, London W12 8AW
Tel: 020 8740 2270   Fax: 202 8740 2280

Text © Louis Fidge and Ray Barker

Illustrations © Phil Burrows, Richard Duszczak, David Lock, Tim Oliver, John Plumb, Sylvie Poggio Artists Agency and Ken Vail Graphic Design (Liz Bryan)

Designed by Ken Vail Graphic Design, Cambridge

British Library Cataloguing-in-Publication Data
A CIP record for this book is available from the British Library

ISBN: 1 84085 237 2

Printed in the UK by Bath Press Limited

Every effort has been made to trace copyright holders and to obtain their permission for the use of copyright material. The authors and publishers would gladly receive information enabling them to rectify an error or omission in subsequent editions.

Letts Educational is the trading name of BPP [Letts Educational] Ltd